HELP
for a
WINTER BIRD

**Nature study for
beginning readers**

This book belongs to

A Gift From

Winter

A Winter Bird

Chickadee

Birds need food
in the winter.

All birds need food in winter.

Here is food for
a bird.

There is food
for a bird

You can help birds
get more food.

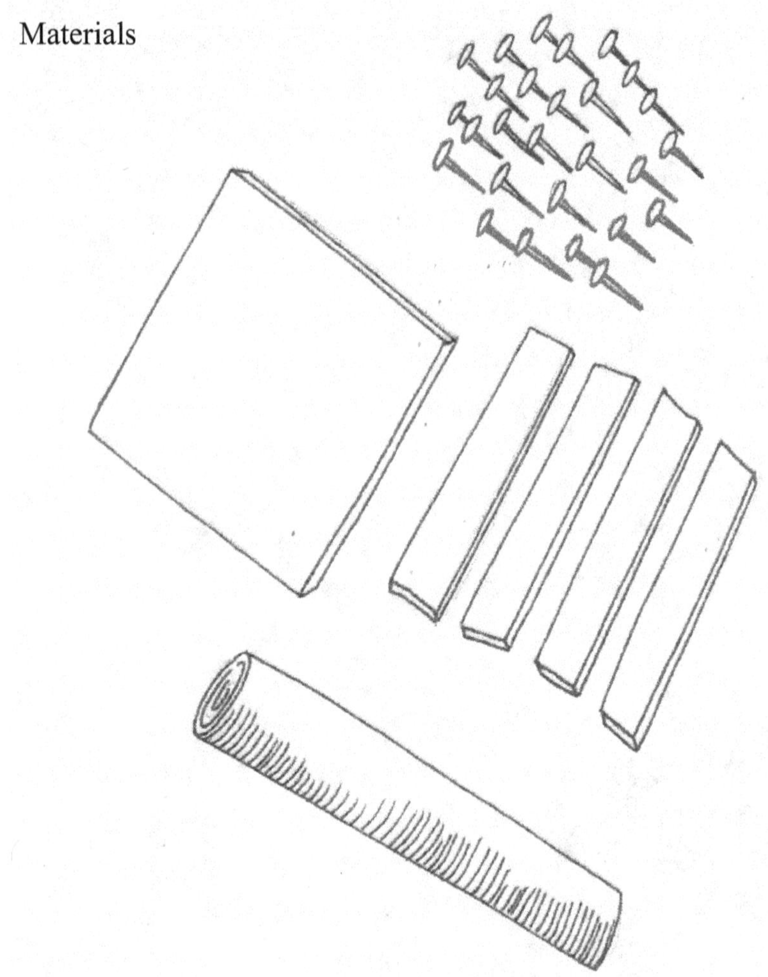

You can help the birds get more food in the winter by making a food tray.

The food tray.

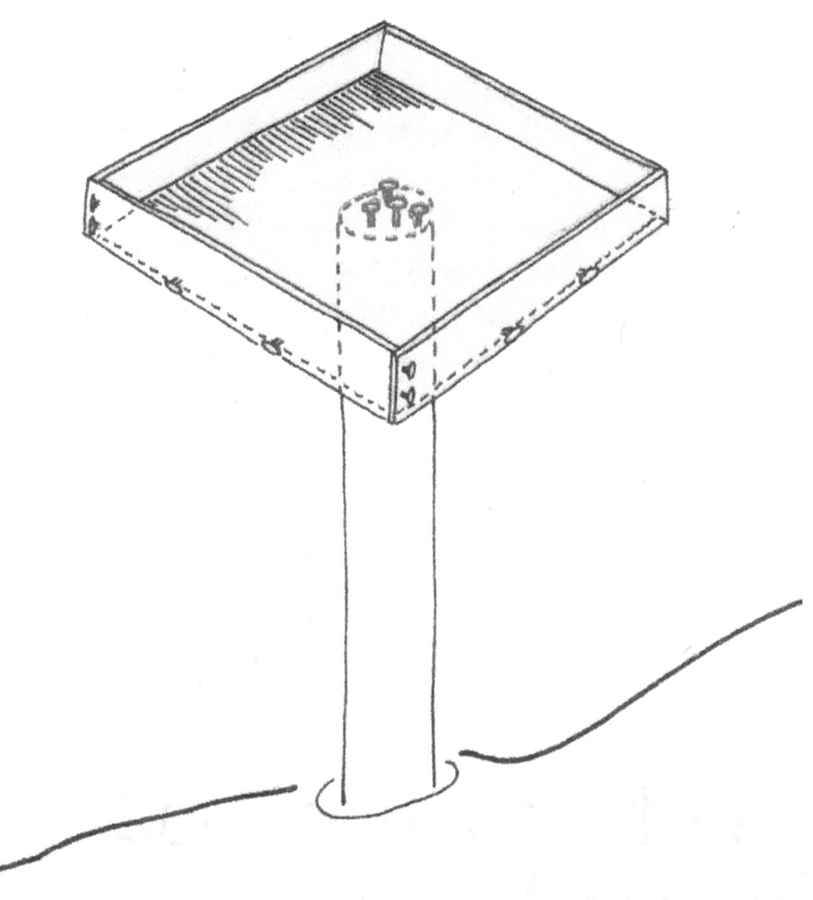

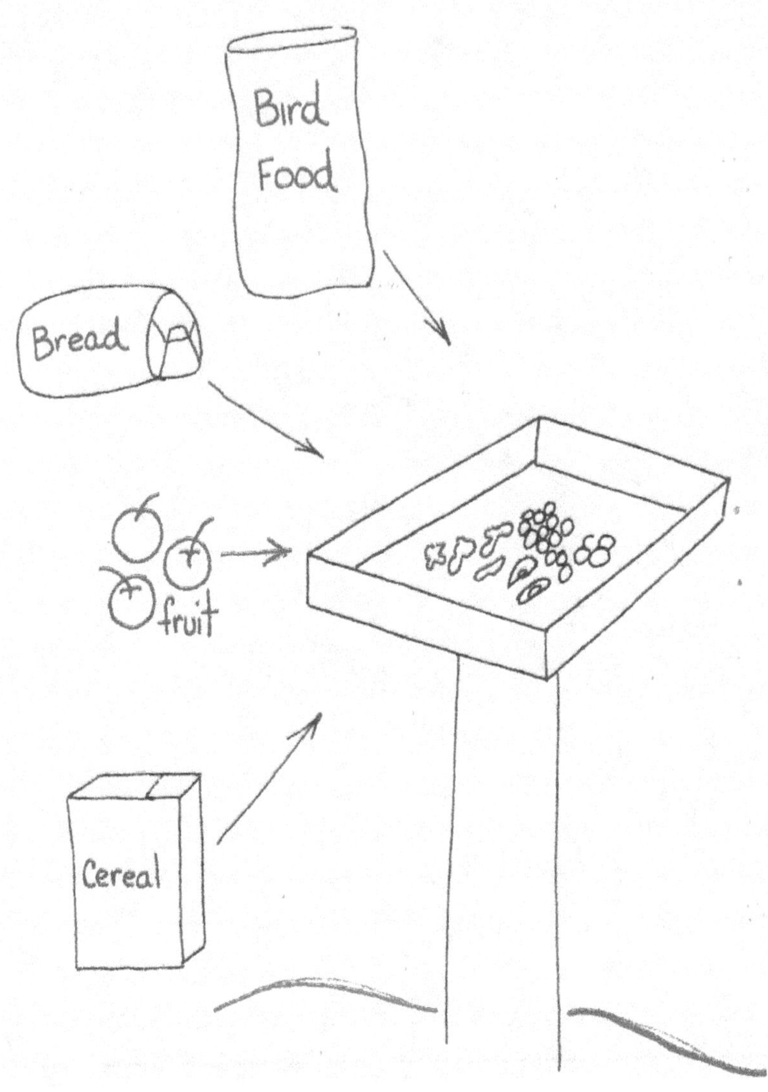

Put food in the food
tray for the birds.

Or you can set up
a tube feeder for the
birds.

Put food in the tube feeder for the birds.

The birds will come to your bird feeder.

Watch how many birds come to your bird feeder.

Watch a bird come to your feeder.

Put food in your bird
feeder every day.

Count the birds that come to your feeder.

How many birds came
to your bird feeder
today?

Happy Winter Birds.

The End

Learning Words

a	help	up
all	how	will
bird	in	you
birds	is	your
by	making	watch
can	many	winter
came	more	
come	need	
count	or	
day	put	
every	set	
end	that	
feeder	the	
food	there	
for	tray	
get	to	
happy	today	
here	tube	

Graphic courtesy of John F. Gardner

Do you have a bird food tray or tube feeder in your yard ? If you do; how may of the birds that came to your bird feeder can you name ?

____ Northern Cardinal
____ American Goldfinch
____ Dark-eyed Junco
____ House Finch
____ Grosbeak
____ Siskin
____ Black-capped Chickadee
____ Blue Jay
____ Downy Woodpecker
____ Mourning Dove

____ House Sparrow
____ European Starling
____ White-breasted Nuthatch
____ Tufted Titmouse
____ Common Grackle
____ Red-bellied Woodpecker
____ Hairy Woodpecker